Library of Congress Cataloging-in-Publication Data available.

ISBN: 978-0615988948

Manufactured in the USA.

MEET SCOTT ALEXANDER

Leadership and martial arts expert Scott Alexander works with individuals and organizations to improve their impact. As a speaker, coach, and consultant, Scott is adept at meeting people where they are and pushing them to the next level of performance.

A 5th Degree Black Belt, Scott is a Master Instructor with Golden Knights Karate and has owned a small business for over two decades. With a master's degree in psychology from Boston College, he honed his skills as a leader working in both large and small organizations in C-level positions.

Scott draws on his experiences in martial arts and business to challenge people and organizations to be principle-driven in order to maximize their impact.

Lead Like a Black Belt

MORE PRAISE FOR LEAD LIKE A BLACK BELT

*"**Lead Like a Black Belt** shows how to apply lessons from the dojo to leading people in the workplace, the classroom and the world of sports. Like an effective kick, Scott's book is powerful, intense and right on target. You won't find a formula for overnight success, but if you have the vision and the discipline, you will find greater understanding and compelling new insight. **Lead Like a Black Belt** delivers all the wisdom of martial arts…with none of the bruises."*

–MARTY WEEDON, MARYLAND STATE POLICE (RET'D)
6TH DEGREE MASTER BLACK BELT

*"Scott's approach to leadership development in **Lead Like a Black Belt** is a breath of fresh air. Comparing the steps a martial arts student takes on the path to Black Belt with the phases a growing leader must pass through to create maximum impact was a fascinating and compelling study—one that prompted me to reflect on my own personal leadership style, and the lessons I've learned along the way. Scott's passion and intensity for the subject matter comes through loud and clear—I found it to be a captivating read!"*

–CAROL EATON, PH.D.
PRESIDENT, DAYTONA STATE COLLEGE

"Scott Alexander relies on his significant experience in the business arena, and his more than thirty years in the martial arts, to weave the art of karate into the science of leadership. He staunchly resists modeling his thoughts after the popular "checklist" format, instead letting each of his guiding principles unfold fully and with intention. He has mindfully pulled out "nuggets of wisdom" throughout the text of the book, graphically presenting them so that they reinforce the content. This is a nimble, original comparison of two unique arenas that will give you a principle-driven gauge to assess your own evolution as a leader."

–KYLE JORDAN
MANAGING DIRECTOR, ACCENTURE

For all my students and colleagues –
We have accomplished much on our path together.

TABLE OF CONTENTS

"THE ULTIMATE AIM OF THE ART OF KARATE LIES NOT IN VICTORY OR DEFEAT, BUT IN THE PERFECTION OF THE CHARACTER OF ITS PARTICIPANTS."

–GICHIN FUNAKOSHI

PROLOGUE

When The Student Was Ready...

In 1983, I walked through the doors of a martial arts training center for the first time.

I was 18 years old.

I didn't know it yet, but I was about to embark on one of the most significant and formative experiences of my life.

Always a fan of Chuck Norris, I was ready to exchange my eight-year football career for the ancient battle arts. I had decided to leave the gridiron for the *dojo*, and embrace the world of the Karate Kid.

So I hung up my jersey, and put on the *gi*—the traditional uniform of karate.

No more cleats on the grass.

Only bare feet on a hardwood floor.

No more team.

Only me.

I was ready.

...the Teacher Appeared

Once inside the *dojo*, I learned the physical side of martial arts quickly. I was young and I was flexible. My natural athleticism, along with the work I'd done in football camp honing my skills as a kicker, translated well to the movements I was learning as a martial artist.

Shortly thereafter, I found my way to the Golden Knights Karate Club and Master Marty Weedon, a nationally ranked martial arts expert.

Marty proved to be a talented teacher, but not in the traditional sense of the word. He didn't break down moves and demonstrate the steps sequentially. He didn't explain much verbally. He simply had remarkable natural ability, and he led with his extraordinary gift: fighting.

Six days a week for six years, I worked out alongside him and a host of other talented students. Quite often, I went on the road with him, watching him compete against other nation-

dojo: *noun.* Refers to a formal training place for students of martial arts.

sensei: *noun.* Refers to a senior karate instructor.

gi (gee): *noun.* A two-piece garment worn by martial artists, consisting of loose-fitting pants and a wraparound jacket.

kata: *noun.* A series of techniques and stances performed from memory to demonstrate mastery of form, power, and intensity.

ally ranked Black Belts. Little by little, I began to understand what exactly it was about his unconventional style that made him great.

The most important thing I realized was this: martial arts was not something Marty Weedon did. Being a martial artist was simply who he was.

For him, the ancient art was not a series of moves or techniques that he could dissect, master and then teach others. He had the uncanny ability to make the movements completely and intrinsically his own.

I also observed repeatedly that he had a remarkable ability to evaluate any situation with lightning speed, and respond immediately in a powerful, focused way. When confronted with an opponent on the attack, he knew what his body should do. And he could always make it perform instantly, precisely, and with tremendous power.

Although the term "spar" has been used for years in relation to two combatants practicing their art, at Golden Knights we prefer the term "fight." Our reputation is partially based on the fact that we are a "fighting" school, so the term represents a proud tradition. The term is not derogatory; rather, it reflects our emphasis on the practical application of techniques.

Finally, I've never met anyone with a greater ability to stay absolutely grounded in the present moment. From his attack to his defense to the eventual takedown, Marty always did the right thing, at the right time, in the right order, for the right result.

It was an extraordinary thing to watch.

After years and years of *doing*, Marty Weedon had crossed over into the realm of *being*.

Think of it this way: every martial artist works hard at a series of movements and techniques, and eventually his ability to execute them becomes part of him. But for many, these abilities are like a transplanted organ or a skin graft. The abilities may have become part of the practitioner, but the art is still separate. For masters like Marty Weedon, it's a different story. Martial arts becomes literally tattooed on their DNA.

This *being* versus *doing* gave him a charismatic presence that was not only inspiring but instructional in a very different way. I have become the martial artist that I am because of a perfect storm of factors—but it all began, and remains firmly rooted in, my exposure to Marty Weedon.

And So It Begins

I earned my Black Belt in 1990, the same year I achieved my Master's Degree in Psychology. My two parallel goals—for a Black Belt and an advanced degree—converged at virtually the same time.

What a coincidence.

Or maybe not.

After graduation, I began my career in psychology. I also married my long-time girlfriend, started saving for a house, and contemplated the idea of one day starting a family.

Evenings and weekends, however, I continued my dedication to martial arts, competing against other Black Belts, performing demonstrations, and assisting with classes at Golden Knights.

Soon after earning my Black Belt, I was offered the opportunity that would prove to be the gateway for the next important phase of my journey as a martial artist and as a leader. The principal of a local private school asked Marty to teach a class on campus. Because his schedule wouldn't permit the extra commitment, Marty recommended that I take on this new endeavor.

I was honored that my respected teacher thought I was ready for this next leg of my journey. However, as a new Black Belt, I was firmly entrenched in the role of student. Initially, it was hard to see myself as a teacher.

Teaching ignited something inside me that I didn't understand at the time. It would be years before I would realize what it was about the process that was so energizing. But more about that later...

One thing was crystal clear from the beginning: teaching students made me more aware than ever of how much I still had to learn. I began to train at Golden Knights with more dedication than ever before.

Over the next 15 years, participation in my class grew, and my students were growing and achieving. My wife and I had two children, and my professional career was moving forward. I was promoted to chief operating officer of a division within a large, statewide organization.

In 2007, I was asked to lead the start-up of an innovative non-profit with the potential to have an unprecedented impact on the lives of children and families in the local community. As the CEO, my position involved hiring and training a staff and a board of directors, educating local politicians and members of other organizations, and working extensively with the community to solve a complex societal challenge.

Over the years, each consecutive job required me to give more and more of myself.

More problem-solving.

More collaboration.

More leadership.

Simultaneously, I was also working on my evolution as a martial artist. Unlike my mentor, my identity as a martial artist was emerging not as a fighter or a competitor, but as a teacher—a sensei, if you will.

It was no longer about me as a martial artist. Instead, it was about me as an instructor, responsible for bringing someone else along the path of becoming a Black Belt.

In fact, promoting my first student to Black Belt was simultaneously a huge accomplishment and an astounding revelation to me…

…AND THAT'S WHEN IT HIT ME

An important part of the Black Belt test is the student essay. Each candidate is asked to write a paper answering one simple question: What does it mean to be a Black Belt?

I had been working with these students for several years. We spoke often about their challenges and achievements, and I thought I knew them well.

But I was not prepared for how profound their answers were, or how deeply they would affect me.

In fact, here are some quotes from the Black Belt papers of my students:

> *"Being a Black Belt does not mean that I am perfect, but that I have the discipline to do what is right. I set an example to those I know and meet by doing so. I work hard, try my best, and take responsibility for my actions."* –RACHEL, AGE 13

> *"By the time one reaches the stage of Black Belt, they should have achieved a state of emotional preparedness.…They should display*

confidence in their abilities, but not to the point of arrogance. A Black Belt knows their limits and strives to overcome them through practice." –ALEXANDRA, AGE 15

"One of the most important things about being a Black Belt is making the best of every situation. When in a bad situation, a Black Belt would not hesitate to do whatever is right…it is a status that you have to work hard to earn, and once you earn it, you have to live by it. A Black Belt should be an inspiration to all people." –RUHEE, AGE 14

How could such wisdom come from such young people?

Over the years, every Black Belt paper (regardless of the age of the student) contained these themes.

And that's when it hit me…

All these years that I had been working with my students to develop them into Black Belts, something less obvious but just as profound had been happening simultaneously: they were training to be leaders in the truest sense of the word.

Bottom line: Everything my students were learning inside the *dojo* could—and should—cross over into "the real world." Mastery of the concepts outlined in this book that shape the evolution of a martial artist on the way to Black Belt create an effective path for any developing leader to follow.

And that's where the concept of ***Black Belt Leadership*** was born.

THE HARDEST THING TO DO AS A BLACK BELT BOTH INSIDE AND OUTSIDE KARATE IS TO STAND FOR THE BELIEFS THAT COME WITH THE TIGHTLY SEWN PIECE OF COTTON (THE BELT). IN SITUATIONS OF PEER PRESSURE, TEMPTATION, AND MORAL AMBIGUITY, YOU MUST UPHOLD THESE PRINCIPLES. OTHERWISE YOU LESSEN THE SIGNIFICANCE OF EACH AND EVERY OTHER INDIVIDUAL WHO WEARS A BLACK BELT.

–MACKENSIE "BIG MAC" SMITH, 1ST DEGREE BLACK BELT

INTRODUCTION

Part Science, Part Art

It's easy to tell when a good leader is at work.

A gifted leader gets the "right" people to do the "right" things at the "right" time. When there is conflict, great leaders guide us through a process that allows us to reach even greater heights. We are focused on the future and all the promise it holds. We are inspired to perform at our best.

Conversely, it's just as easy to tell when a poor leader is at the helm.

Unfortunately, it is more likely that we've experienced this less inspired type of leadership. Under these conditions, relationships and emotions take precedence over good decisions. Past transgressions determine present actions, and the future doesn't look so good. Conflict is intensified as it presents an opportunity for past wrongs to be vindicated. No one is motivated to perform above the bare minimum necessary.

We may be able to recognize the effects of good leadership, but nailing down why one person is a good leader and another is not is a different story.

What is it about leadership that makes it so hard to define and create in the moment?

It is because the ability to lead—like most human characteristics—is a mixture of traits we are born with and skills that we acquire. Because leadership, much like karate, is part science and part art.

Most modern theories about leadership development focus exclusively on the "skill acquisition" portion of this equation. The assumption is that anyone who reads the "right" books, takes the "right" classes and implements the "right" strategies can become an effective leader.

Why is it that we don't have any problem with the idea that people are born with other traits, but the idea of a "knack" for leadership is not considered to be one of them?

This emphasis on learned skills excludes an important variable: the capacity for leadership—at least in part—comes from certain traits that are part of our personalities from birth.

At birth, nature (our parents' DNA) imprints on each of us a set of certain qualities. Think of this bundle of traits as something that is uniquely yours—like your fingerprint, or your signature.

As we mature, certain of these characteristics are either enhanced or ignored, but the innate fingerprint remains the same.

As we enter adulthood, we all have strengths that, hopefully, lead us to vocational and recreational activities that allow us to feel competent and fulfilled.

However, because the fingerprint remains the same, sometimes we stumble onto hidden talents that we didn't know we had. They were always there, just undiscovered.

This is how the retired bank president "suddenly" discovers at age 68 that she has a "knack" for painting. Nature gave her this talent at birth; now that she has time to nurture it, it blooms.

Our "knack" for leadership is a cluster of traits that make up our natural inclination to lead including charisma, intelligence, appearance, stature and voice tone. In martial arts, that cluster of traits includes things like aggressiveness, flexibility, height and bulk.

Blossoming into the leader we want to be requires us to master skills according to our unique strengths and deficits—but we've got to know where to start!

New students are coming into my class all the time. As I watch them work through the early levels of movement, one of the things I am evaluating is their degree of flexibility.

As you might imagine, I have seen hundreds of students, and each has what is immediately apparent as a very specific level of flexibility. In my 30 years of training, I have never witnessed new students who are naturally *inflexible* become extremely *flexible*.

With hard work, do they become more flexible? Yes! Do they ever catch up with the students who are naturally flexible? Absolutely not. Does that make them lesser martial artists? Not necessarily…

In fact, it may make them even better martial artists.

But more on that later.

Know Thyself

Each of us has a genetic fingerprint—a blueprint of skills and deficits. When we understand our raw materials, we can determine our starting point on the road to success. We can't change our individual genetic inclinations; however, if we are willing to work hard enough, we can develop skills that will allow us to accomplish anything.

> BLACK BELTS MUST KNOW THEIR OWN LIMITATIONS IN ORDER TO PERFECT AND SURPASS ANY LIMITATIONS.
>
> –DANIEL, BLACK BELT CANDIDATE

Leadership, much like martial arts, requires us to submit to an **all-encompassing process or journey**. It starts with our innate abilities, and transforms us as we move along the path from *doing* to *being*. Because it is all encompassing, the journey requires us to use our talents to overcome our shortcomings.

Great leaders don't simply accept their circumstances; they transcend them.

Great leaders tap into internal resources to harness external factors, and transform their situations.

Take Jimmy Buffett. (Yeah, I know—not the first name that comes to mind when thinking about leadership, but bear with me).

> ## A MAN'S GOT TO KNOW HIS LIMITATIONS
>
> –"DIRTY HARRY" CALLAHAN

Here's a singer who admits publicly that he doesn't have the greatest voice—arguably the most important trait to become a performer. But he used his impressive gift for story-telling, and his knack for putting on a show to make up for his shortcomings. He crafted a new genre of music that has lasted through five decades—not too bad for a guy without a stellar voice.

It is possible to leverage natural gifts in such a way as to overcome any deficits and increase the ability to lead others capably regardless of where the genetic starting point is.

In fact, great leaders emerge when nature provides the means and experience provides the opportunity.

The purpose of this book is to help enhance your leadership ability, wherever it lies on the spectrum, and to give strategies and ideas that will help maximize the effectiveness of your unique blueprint of leadership traits.

Using This Book

This book is intended for leaders of all types, including:

- Parents stepping into volunteer coaching positions for their kids' teams

- People stepping into leadership positions at work

- Seasoned leaders who are looking to push their limits and break through to the next level

In essence, this book provides a framework for understanding what it takes to cultivate leadership for any aspiring leader in any arena—no matter where your genetic starting point is.

It is broken down into concepts gleaned from more than 30 years in martial arts training and leadership positions including CEO, COO, coach, therapist, and board member.

Early versions of this book contained chapters, each covering a principle common to both Black Belt training and leadership development.

While convenient, this approach proved too restrictive. Everything is related. Several concepts work hand-in-glove with each other, and others—one in particular—permeate everything from start to finish.

Sometimes the neatest solutions aren't the best ones.

So I went back to the drawing board, and organized the information differently.

Instead of a dozen chapters, there are three sections: the Emerging Leader, the Competent Leader, and the Transformational Leader.

Martial arts students move through levels signified by belt colors.

Similarly, leaders go through stages as well.

Their journey is a progression from emerging to competent to transformational leadership.

In essence, both martial artists and leaders proceed along a pathway from *doing* to *being*.

BEING A BLACK BELT MEANS THAT I HAVE TAKEN LIFE LESSONS FROM ALL THE YEARS OF PRACTICE... AND I CARRY WHAT I'VE LEARNED WITH ME EVERY DAY. KARATE HAS BECOME A PART OF WHO I AM AND WHAT I'LL BECOME IN THE FUTURE.

–RACHEL, BLACK BELT CANDIDATE

It's the difference between someone who practices martial arts, and a person who *is* a martial artist.

Likewise it's the difference between a person who has leadership responsibilities and someone who *is* a leader.

THE JOURNEY OF 1,000 MILES...

...begins with a single step. At least that's how the saying goes.

> THE TEST OF A GOOD TEACHER IS NOT HOW MANY QUESTIONS HE CAN ASK HIS PUPILS THAT THEY WILL ANSWER READILY, BUT HOW MANY QUESTIONS HE INSPIRES THEM TO ASK HIM WHICH HE FINDS IT HARD TO ANSWER.
>
> –UNKNOWN

There are two important messages here: first, just make a beginning—start somewhere. The second is, once you make that beginning, don't be fooled—there is a long and, at times, arduous road ahead.

Yet if you open any browser on your computer you are bound to find several articles along the lines of "10 Steps to…" do just about anything better. Everyone is looking for a shortcut. And unfortunately, this has been done with leadership over and over again—reducing a complex journey to a handful of simple steps.

This book starts after you've completed those "10 simple steps."

In other words, you won't find a magic formula for making yourself a better leader in these pages. Instead, you will find principles and concepts gleaned from years of experience. Each concept is developed using

AS YOU READ,
PAY SPECIAL
ATTENTION TO
THE HIGHLIGHTED
INFORMATION IN
THE WEDGE-SHAPED
BOXES ON THE RIGHT
AND LEFT OF THE
PAGES.

THESE "NUGGETS OF
WISDOM" ARE TRULY THE
TAKE-AWAYS FROM THIS
BOOK. WHEN COMBINED
WITH YOUR UNIQUE
DNA FINGERPRINT,
THEY WILL GUIDE
YOUR GROWTH.

several key *principles* that are specifically cultivated in martial arts training.

As you read, pay special attention to the highlighted information in the wedge-shaped boxes on the right and left of the pages. These "Nuggets of Wisdom" are truly the take-aways from this book. When combined with your unique DNA fingerprint, they will guide your growth.

My sincere hope is that this book makes you **ask more questions**. By asking questions, we continually seek answers and that leads us to new understandings.

The following principles are the building blocks for the concepts throughout this book. They are the cornerstones on the path to Black Belt.

RESPECT

The very first thing a martial arts student learns is to bow at the door of the *dojo*, bow to the instructor, and bow to an opponent before engaging in any level of activity. Even the newest White Belt knows that these simple actions reflect respect—and respect underpins everything that is done in martial arts. From our first encounter to the last, respect is the bedrock of everything we do.

CONFIDENCE

Trying new things, such as engaging a new opponent, can be extremely instructional. How that interaction unfolds can either build a student's confidence, or deflate it significantly—using conventional wisdom, it all depends on whether he or she "wins" or "loses." This all changes, however, when students begin to understand that learning—not winning—is the goal of every encounter. Once students believe this at a core level, they can never really "lose" again. And nothing can shake their confidence.

FLEXIBILITY

Flexibility refers to the body's ability to bend and stretch. But it also refers to the mind's ability to change the way we look at things based on new information or challenges that present themselves.

> EACH PRINCIPLE IS MEANT FOR A REASON, WHETHER IT BE TO RESPECT OTHERS OR SHOW SELF CONTROL, THESE MORAL PRINCIPLES ARE THE DIFFERENCE....
>
> –ANDY, BLACK BELT CANDIDATE

For example, early in my martial arts training, I hit a bump in the road. It had to do with fighting. I was not especially aggressive by nature, and I wasn't particularly comfortable with combat. Unlike other students whose tendencies were to rush in and attack, I hung back. There were moments during that time when I wondered if I had hit the wall that would keep me from earning my Black Belt. As I grew in flexibility, however, I learned to change the way I looked at fighting, and adapted my approach to fit my strengths.

FOCUS

More than anything else, martial arts teaches you the importance of focus. A student standing across from someone with gloves on who is about to attack learns very quickly to be 100 percent in the moment. A student training to be a Black Belt must learn how to tune out all distractions in order to be laser-focused on demand. A combination of exacting body awareness—down to minute details of stance and posture—and a keen mental concentration results in a level of focus that is remarkably powerful.

DISCIPLINE

"Doing the RIGHT thing, even when no one is looking" is the essence of discipline. Skipping just one class can lead to taking a week—even a month—off, and that is time that the student never gets back. And when the student returns—if indeed he does—he will find that he can't pick up where he left off. He has gone backwards, and his colleagues have moved ahead. The cumulative effect is loss of opportunity, and a diversion from what he wants to accomplish. The only way to move forward is to be there.

BALANCE

Like flexibility, this quality has a literal and a figurative application. Physically, you must learn balance so that you can kick, throw, punch and fight without falling. Quite literally, if I lose my balance, the fight is lost. Balance, however, also refers to emotional equilibrium. When the student is out of emotional balance, it is impossible to find the focus needed to move forward. This is when we learn to make peace with what is affecting our stability and then come back, ready to work.

CONTROL

The basic forms and sets of movements we learn in martial arts are hundreds of years old. They contain opportunities to practice controlling our bodies. They instruct us in how to position our feet, heads, hands, and extremities. Their lessons are not immediately obvious, but when we go to fight someone, it is immediately clear: fighting is all about controlling yourself. And by controlling yourself, you control the fight.

MOMENTUM

Momentum is created by the appropriate alignment of hands, hips, and stances. If I manage my momentum and my opponent's properly, I will gain the advantage. Sometimes small adjustments create huge shifts in momentum. With minimal movement, I can get someone to react significantly. Being able to create momentum allows a student to change the flow of the fight. It changes the tide of an interaction.

INDOMITABLE SPIRIT

Contrary to popular opinion, excellence in martial arts isn't only about the height and power of the kick, or the precision of the forms and movements. *The mental or spiritual nature of martial arts is equally important and proves to be far more elusive.*

One of the most important factors in progressing to the level of Black Belt is the development of what we call the indomitable spirit. This is when the student moves from drawing on her physical reserves to leveraging her individual spirit in order to keep going. Learning to "never give up" is a watershed moment in the journey to black belt.

And it is a lesson that one never forgets.

KARATE BELT COLORS

Karate schools use a belt coloring system to signify levels or stages of achievement.

White: Signifies birth, or beginning of the life cycle. Think of a seed beneath the snow in winter. A White Belt student is a beginner searching for knowledge of the art.

Yellow: Signifies the first beams of sunlight which shine upon the seed, giving it new strength. A Yellow Belt student receives first rays of knowledge from his instructors.

Green: Signifies the growth of the seedling as it transforms into a plant. A Green Belt student strengthens and refines her techniques.

Blue: Signifies the blue sky as the seed sprouts from the earth and begins to grow. The Blue Belt student is fed additional knowledge of the art in order for his body and mind to continue to grow and develop.

Brown: Signifies the ripening of the seed, a maturing and harvesting process. A Brown Belt is an advanced student whose techniques are beginning to mature. She is beginning to understand the fruits of the path.

Black: Signifies the darkness beyond the sun. A Black Belt student seeks new, more profound knowledge of the art. As he begins to teach others, he plants new seeds and helps them grow and mature. His students blossom and grow through a never-ending process of self-improvement, knowledge, and enlightenment

THE
EMERGING
LEADER

Now What?

You've been asked to coach your child's sports team or take on a new leadership position at work. Now what?

Experience has just handed you an opportunity for new skills to emerge and for your leadership to move toward the next level.

Priority number one: break through any pre-conceived notions and learn to create results by harnessing confidence, focus, and momentum.

WAX ON, WAX OFF

When most of us call to mind the image of an accomplished martial artist, the picture usually includes an individual breaking a board or a cement block. Whether this "break" is completed using a hand or a foot, the resulting mental picture conjures up the power of karate in one iconic image.

So it's understandable that many think that learning how to break a board is a goal of martial arts in and of itself—a sort of rite of passage, or even an act of bravado.

But that's simply not true.

Breaking a board is not a stunt to be applauded as much as an experience to be learned from.

Dissecting the elements of "breaking" is a concrete way for students of martial arts to recognize and respect the power of ***confidence***, ***focus*** and ***momentum*** in achieving a goal.

Therefore, the goal is never to just break a board, or to help others learn how to break. Rather, the exercise of "breaking" is done to illuminate a basic principle of martial arts: when *confidence*, *focus* and *momentum* come together, the board breaks.

There are strong parallels between *breaking* in martial arts and effective leadership.

Let's examine what it takes to yield the type of power that causes a board to break and how it applies to effective leadership.

GREAT LEADERS EMERGE WHEN NATURE PROVIDES THE MEANS AND EXPERIENCE PROVIDES THE OPPORTUNITY.

−SCOTT ALEXANDER

Confidence

At the core of the ability to break is confidence.

It's important to keep in mind that true confidence doesn't have anything to do with an inflated sense of self. Rather, true confidence is the powerful by-product of the certain knowledge that you have trained yourself carefully and completely, and that you are prepared to handle any challenge that comes your way.

For example, when a new student fights for the first time, he or she will fall into one of two categories: aggressive or passive.

As you might imagine, the aggressive student will rush in and attack. These students generally meet with initial success, because they have an approach that works immediately. At first glance, this looks like an inarguable strength.

On the other hand, passive students don't know where to begin. Being a little fearful of the whole experience, they tend to hang back.

But a masterful instructor will help the student turn this initial reticence into strength—a strength so powerful that it might, in fact, allow him to surpass the naturally aggressive student in time.

Think of it this way.

Students without innate fighting ability are likely to be more open to listening to alternatives, giving them a wide repertoire of techniques.

Without a natural "killer instinct" to fall back on, passive students must learn a variety of responses, skills, and strategies, giving them more options to draw from in the arena—ultimately making them more effective.

On the other hand, the naturally aggressive students have a tendency to revert to the one way of fighting and defending that has served them in the past—even if it's not the best choice for the present situation.

CONFIDENCE ISN'T THE ABSENCE OF FEAR...IT'S BEING ABLE TO TAKE ACTION IN SPITE OF FEAR.

At some point in the evolution to Black Belt—usually around Blue Belt—passive students will surpass aggressive students in fighting skills because they have more options available to them, and have learned to adapt their strategies to different circumstances. Once these students have developed confidence and conquered fear, they experience success where they were previously overpowered.

THE DESIRED OUTCOME ISN'T WINNING OR LOSING... ...IT'S LEARNING.

Likewise, the student with an aggressive fighting style gets a lesson in flexibility at this point. Seemingly overnight her less-aggressive peers begin to have answers to her attack strategy. She is no longer able to manage the fight with a singular approach and she's getting hit a lot more. Now it's her turn to experience fear; it's her turn to develop true confidence by practicing and employing multiple strategies.

And in the end, all students must realize that having confidence is not the absence of fear—it's being able to take action in spite of fear, knowing that you are fully trained and able to deal with what is in front of you.

HOW TO WIN EVERY TIME

How do two Black Belts fight each other and both come away with their confidence intact?

While both competitors want to win, Black Belts have trained themselves to think about the encounter differently.

In the Black Belt tradition, encounters are not about winning and losing. That's because we have taught ourselves to view every engagement as a learning experience. Our goal is to come away from every encounter having learned something new.

This is a powerful notion.

Once you understand that the best outcome of any encounter isn't winning—it's learning—you cannot lose.

You will "win" every time.

Nothing can shake your confidence.

In every sparring session, there are fleeting moments of triumph and defeat. Students on the path to Black Belt learn to revel in the triumph, but to value the defeat as well—because that is where the learning occurs.

Remember: the desired outcome isn't winning or losing. It's learning.

Truly adapting this view of every contest, every encounter, and every experience is a game changer.

Once you understand that learning is the ultimate goal, you will never look at anything in quite the same way again.

As leaders, we build confidence through this same process. We may not always make the playoffs, and we may not always make the sale. We won't win every bid, every grant, or every job we apply for—but if we use that "loss" as a springboard for learning, we will win every time.

WHEN WE CHANGE OUR THINKING, WE CONTROL OUR ACTIONS.

BY CONTROLLING OUR ACTIONS, WE CHANGE OUR CIRCUMSTANCES.

This sort of confidence is charismatic. When a leader exhibits the type of confidence gained in this manner, it draws people together rather than separates them. It intrigues them, it engages them, and it moves us all forward in a powerful way.

When we change our thinking, we control our actions.

By controlling our actions, we change our circumstances.

FIGHTING SMARTER, NOT HARDER

Every martial artist remembers the day he first watched an older, more experienced fighter take down a younger, more powerful opponent. It's an eye-opener to many, because it's the first time they understand the power of self-control in the ring.

The reason an opponent with less physical capacity can triumph over the quicker, stronger opponent is because the more experienced opponent refuses to engage in the match on the other fighter's terms. He doesn't contest that he is physically outmatched, so he focuses on rendering that advantage meaningless. Instead, he relies on a broad array of tools to unbalance his opponent. He doesn't try to overpower.

Rather, he seeks to undermine. He strikes with less force than his opponent—but he applies it where, when, and how it will have the greatest effect. In short, by controlling his approach and his actions, the older, more seasoned fighter controls the pace and the outcome of the match.

Focus

When you think of a successful, productive person, what comes to mind?

Many of us picture a busy person juggling a half dozen important roles simultaneously—perhaps an executive listening in on a conference call while processing email, confirming appointments for the next day, keeping an eye on the home front through text messages from the kids, and keeping abreast of up-to-the-minute news through the latest apps on her smart phone.

Meet the masters of multitasking—those enviable dynamos who seem to be able to do it all simultaneously.

How can they keep all those balls in the air with such grace and precision?

The answer is they can't.

When it comes to the brain's ability to pay attention, the latest research is soundly debunking the myth of multitasking.

It turns out that human beings, say the field's foremost scientists, are biologically incapable of processing more than one "attention-rich input" at the same time.

It can't be done.

Think of it this way: the brain focuses on concepts sequentially, not simultaneously. In order to move onto the next topic, the brain must disengage from one activity *completely* in order to engage in the next. And it takes several tenths of a second for the brain to make each switch.

In fact, multitasking can reduce productivity by up to 40 percent according to some researchers.

Yet, in spite of the statistics, the temptation to multitask has never been greater. Computers are more portable than ever before, and our smart phones are increasingly powerful and ever more present.

Because the ability to achieve at high levels is a function of individual discipline, it's important to fine tune one's ability to perform with control and intention.

In fact, when I introduce a new concept with my martial arts students, we often start by training the students' non-dominant side.

This is to force students out of their comfort zones.

Asking students to work with the hand, arm, foot or leg that is not their preferred one is a simple way to encourage them to get off autopilot and look at things differently.

This moves them to a place of higher concentration and greater intention.

WHEN WE LEAVE OUR COMFORT ZONE, WE BECOME MORE FOCUSED.

BEING CONFUSED OR UNSURE CAN BE A GOOD THING.

EMBRACE OPPORTUNITIES TO BE CONFUSED.

WORK IN SHORT BURSTS OF INTENSE FOCUS.

TRAIN YOUR BRAIN

Examples of how multitasking impairs performance abound—in scholarly research, in the blogosphere and throughout our personal lives.

Why?

Because multitasking whittles away the very core of productivity: focus.

That's why one of the most important concepts a leader in the Black Belt tradition trains themselves to do is to work in short bursts of intense focus.

Let's take a look at some examples from martial arts that illustrate the importance of focus.

As an instructor, I know that there are eight different components and combinations to a basic round kick, a relatively simple maneuver taught in all forms of martial arts—in fact, often the first kick taught to new students.

The only way for a student on the path to Black Belt to achieve an excellent round kick is to focus on each of these individual components and combinations, one at a time.

In order to do a competent kick, the student needs to consider the entire anatomy of the movement.

This is done by focusing on the motion task-by-task, by breaking it down into individual components.

Students study how to set up a kick. They evaluate a variety of stances, and find the one best suited to them.

Then they analyze the position from which the kick is thrown. They start in one position, moving closer to their opponent, and then backing away—assessing the advantages and disadvantages of each position.

Then they dissect the chamber of the kick, and practice it—hundreds and hundreds of times. Next, they add the rotation of the kick, leveraging the back leg first, then the front leg.

Next comes the snap. What do the most powerful kicks look and feel like as the leg snaps in, out and back again?

Each component of the round kick is studied and perfected, one at a time. Over and over again.

Finally, students focus on combining one component with another—for example, the chamber and the snap.

Eventually, they are able to combine all the elements into an entire round kick. The movement is repeated hundreds—maybe thousands—of times.

At some point, after enough rote repetition, the body begins to take over.

LIKE THE
STUDENT
TRYING
TO LEARN
A NEW KICK,
FOCUSING IN ON
THE SMALLEST
PERTINENT DETAIL
OF ANY PROJECT
WITHOUT
DISTRACTIONS
CAN YIELD
ASTOUNDING
RESULTS.

The kick moves from a series of steps the body is imitating to something more transcendent—the kick becomes something the student's body just does, naturally and without thinking.

This can only occur when the student focuses on minute details and trains his body to respond to each one.

The final result is a great kick, but not before each individual component of it has been practiced over and over again with intentional, singular focus.

Like the student trying to learn a new kick, focusing in on the smallest pertinent detail of any project without distractions can yield astounding results.

LEARNING TO FLIP
THE SWITCH

So it seems we've figured out that the ability to do more than one thing at a time doesn't exist.

In addition, we've also learned that switching from one activity to another takes significant brain power—so much so that going from one thing to another all day long adds up to a big loss in focus.

And yet life—both inside the *dojo* and outside—often requires that we handle a variety of activities in a single day...sometimes in a single hour!

So how do we do this effectively?

In helping students along on the path to Black Belt, it starts with what we call "learning to flip the switch."

Learning to flip the switch is one of the most important concepts that a student of martial arts practices. This is the ability that the Black Belt has to move nimbly from one situation to another while retaining focus at all times.

"FLIPPING THE SWITCH IS SOMETHING THAT SHOULD COME NATURALLY TO A BLACK BELT....IT HELPS TO ELIMINATE DISTRACTIONS AND BECOME MORE SUCCESSFUL AT WHATEVER YOU DO."

–RUHEE, BLACK BELT CANDIDATE

For example, martial arts students must be able to move from observing on the sidelines to performing an intricate *kata* on command.

They must be able to go from waiting their turn to performing at their highest level in the ring.

They must develop the ability to move nimbly between a social interaction with a friend to a fight scenario with that same friend (who is now in the role of opponent) when the whistle blows.

This ability to move nimbly and effectively from one situation to another without a loss in focus requires discipline, training and lifelong practice.

To build productive teams, a leader in the Black Belt tradition must encourage people to be able to "flip the switch" at will to assume the role that is needed for maximum results.

This starts by modeling how to do it.

For example, just about everyone in a leadership position has had someone say to them "Do you have five minutes?"

Whether this question comes at a convenient time or not, if you say "yes," whoever is asking has the right to your complete attention.

When a staff member needs a moment of your time and you're expecting a phone call any minute, the answer needs to be "At the moment, no—I'm sorry I don't. When I get off the phone, I'll give you a call and we can talk."

Someone who is trying to process several things at a time will always appear distracted and disinterested. The outcome of such an interaction is far less likely to be positive.

On the other hand, if your answer is "yes," you owe the person in front of you your focused attention—no matter what. It's not possible to truly listen while scrolling through e-mail, straightening piles of paper or answering text messages.

Regardless of how busy you are, let your "yes" be truly "yes." Remove distractions and make eye contact. When you flip the switch in this manner, you set the stage for a positive, focused interaction during which you will ultimately accomplish more than you would have otherwise.

And just as importantly, you model for those around you that it is possible to flip the switch when you need to go from one thing to another.

When we are adept at this skill, it transfers to those we are leading.

For example, consider a person on her way to a sales call who gets a text message from headquarters. The last thing she reads before going into the appointment is "Call me when you get back in the car."

The ability to put the possible ramifications of that message (Am I in trouble? Is there an issue with another client?) out of her mind, and focus completely on the person in front of her is critical in order to build the relationship and make the sale.

The most gifted sales people are said to be those with the ability to clear their minds of distractions and focus completely on the people in front of them.

Likewise, when a martial artist is standing in front of that board or cinder block getting ready to break, she better have flipped the switch.

She better not be thinking of anything else.

Her mind cannot be distracted by what kind of day she had, or what she has to do later on.

LEARN TO FLIP THE SWITCH:

CHANGE YOUR FOCUS QUICKLY, COMPLETELY, AND AT WILL TO MOVE NIMBLY BETWEEN SITUATIONS OR INTERACTIONS.

To break that board, she needs to be 100 percent focused, and completely in the moment.

When fighting another Black Belt, she cannot be thinking about what she looks like to those on the sidelines, or what she feels like having for dinner.

One of the great things about karate is that, should our attention slip even the slightest bit, we receive instant feedback when our opponent painfully "reminds" us of our immediate priority!

Unfortunately, the feedback doesn't surface as quickly in a typical work environment. When that staff person doesn't get your full focus, he will be sure to pass that message along to others on the team. It will take a while, but eventually it will be determined that, although you have an "open door policy," you aren't really available.

Momentum

Sir Isaac Newton pretty much nailed it in 1687 when he first published his laws of motion. The core of his first law is basically this: "a body at rest tends to stay at rest, but a body in motion will stay in motion unless acted upon by an outside force."

Once we've achieved the confidence to begin, and called upon the focus required to move forward, how can we keep outside forces from slowing us down?

What do we need to cultivate so that we can increase our momentum—inside the *dojo*, and in other aspects of our lives?

> TO BE A BLACK BELT, YOU MUST PUSH YOURSELF PAST YOUR PHYSICAL LIMITS. TO BE A BLACK BELT MEANS THAT YOU NEVER GIVE UP ON SOMETHING AND SIMPLY STOP TRYING. I DO THIS NOT ONLY IN KARATE, BUT IN EVERYDAY LIFE. BEING A BLACK BELT MEANS THAT I LIVE MY LIFE WITH DISCIPLINE AND RESPECT.

–KELLY, BLACK BELT CANDIDATE

AN INDOMITABLE SPIRIT

Cultivating what we call an indomitable spirit is the process whereby we learn to dig deep and find reserves we didn't know we had. An indomitable spirit is the means through which we find a way to keep going—always.

THE ONLY WAY TO FAIL IS TO GIVE UP.

At the very end of the test for Black Belt, the student must fight against two instructors. After nearly two hours of performing at the highest level he can manage, the student is put into a situation where he is obviously outmatched. He is physically drained and mentally exhausted.

The purpose of this two-on-one fight is not to ensure that the student can handle two opponents. (Actually, that's covered earlier in the test.) Instead, the point is to see if he can use his brain to make his body continue to work even after the body says "quit."

As an instructor, I am looking for one thing: is the student at the point where he has developed what is needed to fend off the force that would bring him to a halt? Has he cultivated the will to keep going, regardless?

Keep in mind: because the student is worn out and is fighting two fresh opponents above his level of competency, there is no way he can "win" in the traditional sense of the word.

The way the student "wins" is by reaching beyond his physical discomfort and finding reserves of mental energy and emotional strength that will allow him to keep going.

The only way to fail is to give up.

THE
COMPETENT
LEADER

Implementing Tools, Mastering Skills

It typically takes students five years of training to earn the rank of Brown Belt—one step below Black Belt. That's five years of hard work practicing skills and training their bodies—that's thousands of techniques...and stances...and throws...and fights...and *katas*.

> THE DIFFERENCE BETWEEN A BROWN BELT AND BLACK BELT IS ALL IN YOUR HEAD.
>
> –SCOTT ALEXANDER

They have pushed themselves to become more disciplined, more flexible, more balanced, more focused. They hit hard, move quickly, and know what to expect. In short, these students have become competent martial artists.

It takes another two years of training to make the leap from Brown Belt to Black Belt without necessarily learning any new physical skills but rather focusing on the mental side of training.

In much the same way, there is a sub-group of leaders outside the *dojo* who have become effective by implementing tools and mastering skills. These high-performing individuals are capable and have achieved technical proficiency.

But, in order to leverage their expertise to impact others, these leaders must master the next level of concepts.

These are the **Competent Leaders**.

How to Become an Overnight Success...Not!

Author and thought-leader Malcolm Gladwell offered interesting insight into the importance of skill mastery to be successful.

During his research for his groundbreaking book *Outliers*, Gladwell studied the lives of accomplished people to find out how they achieved success.

His conclusion?

All had focused on mastering the skills at the foundation of their fields, and all shared a benchmark in common.

MARTIAL ARTS MYTHS

An old legend claims that early martial artists began their training with a white belt, which eventually became stained black from years of sweat, dirt, and blood. Another story tells of a grand master who never washed his belt, claiming that so doing would wash away the knowledge and experience he had gained on his martial arts.

Each one had invested at least 10,000 hours of practice.

One of his examples involved the Beatles.

You'd have to look long and hard to find anyone who hasn't at least heard of the Beatles, right?

Most people think they burst onto the music scene in 1964 with their first appearance on The Ed Sullivan Show.

But most people are wrong.

The Beatles' "overnight success" actually started in 1960, when the unknown band was cutting their musical teeth on the club circuit in Hamburg, Germany.

The group was underpaid.

The environment was abysmal.

The audiences were unimpressed.

So what did this quartet, whose destiny was to change the face of music as the world knew it, get out of this experience?

Most obviously, they got hours and hours of playing time—in other words, the opportunity to get better.

By 1962, the Beatles were playing eight hours a night, seven days per week.

By 1964, they had played over 1,200 concerts together.

Most bands don't play 1,200 times together in their entire career!

Clearly, like the Beatles of the 1960s, competent leaders can have a great impact on the people around them but it takes a tremendous amount of focused practice.

"IF YOU AIN'T FIRST, YOU'RE LAST."

According to the mantra espoused by Ricky Bobby in the cult classic movie Talladega Nights, "If you ain't first, you're last."

Or are you?

Remember, the value of "winning" in the Black Belt tradition looks different than it does in other contexts.

In the world of sports, many coaches have based their approach on a familiar quote: "Winning isn't everything; it's the only thing."

In the corporate world, managers learn to base their success on what percentage of the market share they are able to capture, or other similar metrics.

Convincing others to buy their product, use their service or invest in their ideas is how they "win."

In the traditional sense, winning is almost always a group effort—it depends on the actions of others.

> # THERE ARE NO LIMITS. THERE ARE ONLY PLATEAUS, AND YOU MUST NOT STAY THERE, YOU MUST GO BEYOND THEM.
>
> –BRUCE LEE

ULTIMATELY, "WINNING" OR "LOSING" IS ARBITRARY— AND ALMOST ALWAYS FLEETING.

However, leaders in the Black Belt tradition—from the locker room to the board room—must embrace a completely different approach to "winning" versus "losing."

The Emerging Leader has redefined "winning" to mean "learning". Moving forward through the martial arts tradition we take this one step further by embracing the idea that one never truly "wins" at anything…as soon as you meet a goal or earn a belt, there is another benchmark to reach.

And there's another thing…students accept that there are negative aspects to every "win" and positive aspects to every "loss," but to be aware of them, they must reflect on things like:

What risks did you take?

How much effort did you expend?

What lessons did you learn?

What did you have to give up in the process?

Was it worth it to take a shot to the midsection so you could deliver a blow to your opponent's head?

Remember, ultimately, "winning" or "losing" is arbitrary—and almost always fleeting.

This is the core of the idea of *yin* and *yang*.

It's a complex idea in Chinese philosophy, but think of it this way: *yin* and *yang* represent the cycle of life.

That which is upwards is *yang*. That which is receding is *yin*.

As a result, the sky, the head, and the top of anything are *yang*. On the other hand, *yin* represents the ground or the earth—the feet and the bottom of anything are *yin*.

The *yin* and *yang* symbol is a circle that has been divided by a symmetrical curve. One half is light, the other half is dark. The light portion of the circle represents *yang* energy. The black portion represents *yin* energy.

Each portion is shaped like a tear drop—full at one end, and thin at the other. The two portions fit seamlessly into each other, illustrating something essential about *yin* and *yang* energy: if you were to cut the circle in half at any point across its circumference, both *yin* and *yang* would be in balance. They are opposites, but they need each other to exist. They are entirely different, but completely dependent.

IN ANY DYNAMIC
INTERACTION—
AT ANY GIVEN
MOMENT—WE ARE
BOTH WINNING
AND LOSING
AT THE
SAME TIME.

Those things which are strong and bright, such as the sun, a campfire, and a candle are all *yang*.

Those things that are soft and receding, such as the night sky, dawn, and water are all *yin*.

When *yang* energy is at its fullest, *yin* energy is just beginning. When *yin* energy is at its fullest, *yang* energy is just beginning. Both *yin* and *yang* require each other to exist—a shadow cannot exist without the light. Where there is *yin*, there is always *yang*. *Yin* and *yang* are constantly changing—evolving from *yin* to *yang* and from *yang* back to *yin*.

This brings to mind another conundrum within the realm of martial arts: the question is not did we "win" or "lose" but what did we gain, and what did we give up in the process?

In any dynamic interaction—at any given moment—we are both winning and losing at the same time.

WHAT DID YOU LEARN?

Chuck Norris famously said that the only fight you ever lose is the one you didn't learn something from. When two Black Belts fight, there are fleeting moments of triumph and defeat throughout. Except in fights to the death, there is rarely an obvious winner or loser.

That's not the point.

The point of the match is to give both opponents ample opportunity to be punched, kicked, and thrown on the ground.

Why?

Because this is where their strengths and areas of weakness will be revealed.

This is how, when, and where they will learn the most.

This is what will get them to the next level of performance.

LOOK FOR THE OPPORTUNITIES TO BE HIT, KICKED, AND KNOCKED TO THE GROUND.

THIS IS WHERE YOU WILL LEARN THE MOST.

The competent leader in the workplace knows that not all projects will move along to fruition with ease. Sometimes, work groups and task forces will get bogged down. Egos will flare and sides will form.

Yet think of it this way: missteps and backfires along the way give people an opportunity to solve problems together for the good of the project. Like soldiers in fox holes, this is where real bonding can happen—and stronger teams will form.

Coaches have a profound opportunity to help build resilience and strength in kids. Yes, we want our young athletes to be competitive and aim to win. But coaches in the Black Belt tradition understand that there's a far greater lesson to be learned.

Consider the scenario of a little girl who—at nine years old—is emerging as a softball powerhouse. She was born with natural athletic ability, and she's been working on fundamentals since her hand was big enough to fit in a glove. It's not unusual for her to spend an hour before practice warming up, and another hour after practice trying to perfect the skills they just worked on. She just has a precocious love of the game, and playing for her—right now, at least—is pure joy.

However, the young player's parents are concerned. The coaches are constantly pointing to their daughter as "the best one on the team." Everything she does is held up to her teammates as the standard to emulate. Their little girl is getting pretty impressed with herself. She's getting a little impatient with her teammates when they make the mistakes new players always will. And while she's busy being critical of others on the team, she's not learning anything of real value.

In the spring, she could move up to the next level of competition, but the coach isn't supporting it. His protégée has helped win a lot of games for him, and he's not eager to give up his prize player.

The young player's parents, however, have made their decision. They feel that, in order for her to grow, she needs more opportunities to "fail." Her base-running won't improve in a league where the "one base on an overthrow" rule still applies, and sliding is still outlawed. Her bat speed and power won't get better until she starts facing more gifted pitchers at the plate. And the mental aspects of the game—her ability to both win and lose with grace—aren't being developed at all.

The coach won't be pleased during spring sign-ups, but this young player will be moving up. She is signing up for a steep learning curve, playing bigger, more experienced kids in an environment that's completely new to her. She won't always be the star, and she'll have to handle making more mistakes than she's used to. But she'll be a better softball player in the end, not in spite of these things but because of them.

THE GREATEST OF THE GREATS

"I've failed over and over and over again in my life. And that is why I succeed." –Michael Jordan

There was a famous Nike commercial years ago featuring Michael Jordan. True, the script was written for him, but it was based on real statistics. "I've missed more than 9,000 shots in my career," he said. "I've lost almost 300 games. Twenty-six times, I've been trusted to take the game winning shot, and I missed. I've failed over and over and over again in my life. And that is why I succeed."

> # I'VE FAILED OVER AND OVER AND OVER AGAIN IN MY LIFE. AND THAT IS WHY I SUCCEED.
>
> –MICHAEL JORDAN

Well stated, Mr. Jordan.

It does take a lot of beatings to grow—on the basketball court, in the *dojo*, and everywhere else.

There's really no way around it.

Those who perform at the highest level of martial arts have gotten to where they are on the continuum because of those who came before them.

They owe their excellence to those who were willing to hit them, kick them, and knock them down, over and over again.

As leaders in the Black Belt tradition, we, too, must embrace these opportunities to be "beaten" in order to maintain our forward momentum.

WHAT DID YOU GIVE UP?

In the journey to master the art of leadership, you will constantly be called upon to adjust.

Sometimes, you will be called upon to re-order your tactics. Other times, it will be necessary to change your approach completely.

Leaders in the Black Belt tradition realize that it's always alright to adjust HOW we are going to get where we're going, but a core principle must never be altered.

Strategies are always fair game, but there is one thing that is non-negotiable: *principles* must never be compromised.

Ever.

For any reason.

This brings to mind dozens of experiences I've had where this has been made crystal clear to me, but I'll share just one.

There was a time when I was asked to lead an emerging non-profit whose mission was to help bring about substantive community change in a suburban area with many challenges.

The population was diverse, and in many ways disenfranchised. Language was an issue for many; money was a problem for most. The risk of failure far outweighed the potential for success.

We created a plan for community outreach, and before long, word had spread that our organization was offering opportunity for kids and support for families. We were working well with the neighborhood schools and businesses. Our pilot after-school program was achieving excellent outcomes, and expansion plans were in the works. We were hosting capacity crowds at our family events. We were getting closer—little by little—to our vision of becoming a "transformational community hub."

We had a long way to go, but we had created significant momentum.

One of our goals was to create a community center, a building that would have room for everything the community needed. But it had to go beyond being accessible to all—we had to actively engage those youth and families who were disengaged. We had to break down social barriers. We could not exclude anyone. Our challenge was to find a way to become financially sustainable as an organization with-

"NEVER PUT PASSION BEFORE PRINCIPLE. EVEN IF WIN...LOSE."

—MR. MIYAGI

COMPROMISE ON STRATEGIES BUT NEVER PRINCIPLES.

out compromising our principle that "no one gets left behind." We could charge fees for our services; however, that would further alienate the very people we were trying to impact.

We started with one strategy, which led to another. And another. And another. You get the idea. As we hit brick wall after brick wall with our plans, we became very flexible. We simply adjusted. We leaned in to every curve that came our way, and figured out a different way.

But the adjustment always had to do with the *how*.

Never the what.

We never compromised on our core principle of actively engaging those most likely to fail.

" IN MATTERS OF STYLE, SWIM WITH THE CURRENT; IN MATTERS OF PRINCIPLE, STAND LIKE A ROCK. "

–THOMAS JEFFERSON

Ultimately, when politics started to take precedence over the mission, that meant walking away from the project—one of the most difficult things I've ever had to do.

But achieving some reduced form of the goal by compromising on principles was never an option. It would have been a hollow victory at best.

Be prepared to compromise on *strategies* but never on *principles*.

Seeking the Big Picture

One of my jobs as an instructor of martial arts is to always seek the big picture.

In other words, in martial arts—and everywhere else—it's the context that counts.

Some call it "getting out of the weeds."

Others refer to it as "the view from 30,000 feet."

Whatever you call it, "seeking the big picture" is an important part of the journey toward creating a leader in the Black Belt tradition.

One day a traveler came across three stonecutters working in a quarry. Each was busy cutting a block of stone. Interested to find out what they were working on, he asked each stonecutter about their task.

The first grumbled, "I am cutting a stone!".

"I am cutting this block of stone to make sure that it's square, and its dimensions are uniform, so that it will fit exactly in its place in a wall," explained the second stonecutter.

The third and happiest of the three replied: **"I am building a cathedral."**

It starts with an understanding that everyone has strengths and weaknesses.

On the field.

At the sales appointment.

Writing a grant.

Fighting in the ring.

We must look at the entire picture instead of getting bogged down in the details.

Details alone are not important. They only matter in relation to the larger picture.

In fact, growth for every one of us is about committing to the total picture.

And being a martial arts instructor challenges me to seek the big picture every day.

When a student is testing for a belt, there are skills that I must evaluate. Not in relation to the other students in class but in relation to the ideal and to that student's potential.

What should that kick look like for a student at this belt level and age?

IT IS THE BIG PICTURE THAT MAKES THE DETAILS RELEVANT.

Is that kick the absolute best she can do?

Am I getting 100 percent of his effort in the ring?

Will it be better in the long run for a student if I reward her efforts right now, or withhold a certain benchmark until she has invested more of herself in the achievement of it?

Backing away from the scenario so I can see the big picture is the only way to arrive at the conclusion that will prove best for that student.

For example, I was recently evaluating two students during a class to determine who was ready for their next test.

One naturally flexible student performed her *katas* accurately and precisely. Apparently born with a knack for fighting, she demonstrated stances, blocks, and strikes that were technically correct and generally superior to her peers. Her demeanor reflected an attitude that seemed remote and dispassionate. She was confident that she had mastered the skills necessary to test for the next belt.

On the other hand, the second student worked through his *katas* with tremendous focus and concentration. While neither as flexible nor as technically proficient as his classmate, he was giving 110 percent—today, and during every class. A quiet young man with a less aggressive nature, he had worked hard on learning a variety of strategies to employ when engaged by an opponent, and was generally adept at selecting the most effective one. But he was adamant that he was not ready to test.

Would it surprise you to learn that I determined that the second student was closer to being ready than his classmate?

While Student #1 had some obvious strengths, she was not performing anywhere near her potential. Student #2 was actually further down the road toward Black Belt. Because I knew him well and was able to put things into a larger context, I was able to discern his initial reticence to test as an indication of his humility and openness toward learning—not a lack of confidence. In short, he was maximizing his talents.

In both these cases, it is the big picture that makes the details relevant.

Outside the *dojo*, making sure you are looking at the big picture is just as important. Even the best idea may make no sense at all when viewed in a larger context.

Think about the non-profit organization whose mission is to create positive and substantive change within a population where alcoholism and its effects are rampant. Even if those involved are not those directly being served, does a pub crawl make sense to raise money for programs and services?

Not if you look at the big picture.

And in a world where avoiding smoking is one of the biggest health challenges facing young people, is a brandy-and-cigar fundraiser for a youth sports league appropriate?

Not when you put the event into context.

The organization may raise some money—sometimes a significant sum. But what the organization is willing to give up—in both these cases, its principles—results in a loss of integrity that represents a far greater loss than the funds raised could ever offset.

Compare Everything to the Ideal

"Shoot for the moon. Even if you miss, you'll land among the stars."

Here is another cliché that would be easy to dismiss if it didn't embody an important truth. Hackneyed though it may be, this saying is the essence of Black Belt thinking.

For the two students mentioned earlier who were preparing to test, consider this: If student #1 is only concerned that her techniques are better than student #2, then she robs herself of the opportunity to get better. She will only work hard enough to be better than her peer but not hard enough to maximize her talents.

Or consider this all-too-familiar conversation in the workplace:

Boss: *"You don't realize how good we have it here. Your problem is that you don't know how bad it is in other places. You need to go visit the other organizations so you can see how good it is here!"*

Employee: *"If I am standing knee deep in mud, and look at the guy who is chest deep in mud, I don't think I have it so bad. But I'm more concerned with finding a way to get out of the mud altogether!"*

This sort of conversation based on dubious logic happens frequently, and illustrates how slippery the slope is from "good enough" to mediocre to downright lackluster.

Unfortunately, the upshot of such flawed thinking leads to this: If, compared to others, we're okay, then why set ambitious goals?

If the general thinking is "we're not so bad," then we don't have to work too hard to maintain our position.

If we're only concerned about where we rank as compared to others, we will settle for mediocrity without even knowing it.

COMPARE EVERYTHING TO THE IDEAL. ONCE WE SETTLE FOR ANYTHING LESS, WE ARE ON A FAST TRACK TO MEDIOCRITY.

BALANCE

The possibility exists that the big picture and the ideal may be at odds. This is when we seek balance.

> BALANCE IS KEY. BALANCE GOOD, KARATE GOOD.... BALANCE BAD, BETTER PACK UP—GO HOME.
>
> —MR. MIYAGI

If we are comparing everything to the ideal, won't we always come up short?

Won't we become perfectionists with all the trappings?

We are striving for the ideal in the context of the big picture.

The student I am evaluating for the next belt will always come up short compared to the ideal student. However, when compared with her capacity, her effort, in the total picture of her personal journey toward perfection, her readiness for advancement becomes clear.

Similarly, as a leader, I know my team's performance will never meet the ideal. But, by taking into account the reality of our current situation and the outcomes we are achieving, our priorities will become clear.

PAYING IT FORWARD

SEEK BALANCE BETWEEN THE BIG PICTURE AND THE IDEAL IN ORDER TO MAKE SENSE OF OUR CURRENT SITUATION AND DETERMINE PRIORITIES.

A martial arts instructor is on a path every day with his students. And from the very beginning, that instructor is sure of one thing: there will come a day when his students will surpass him in skill.

And that's the way it should be.

Unfortunately, not all leaders think this way, do they?

Haven't we all worked for the boss at one time or another who took credit for our work? You know the type. They are usually not very confident people who always seem fearful that something is going to happen to usurp their status or authority.

They are suspicious and worried types—in their minds, there is usually a threat around every corner. If they don't protect themselves, they will be over-thrown in a bloody *coup d'etat*.

With that sort of mindset, it's no wonder that they view anyone with passion and ambition as a threat. The idea of mentoring an employee along a path which might lead them to eventually surpass the boss feels like sheer lunacy.

REALIZING ONE'S OWN POTENTIAL

Somewhere around the time students test for Green Belt, many realize something very important that will influence the rest of their journey to Black Belt.

Excellence is not measured by how well one competes against another, but to what extent he can realize his own potential. In other words, one's biggest competitor is always himself. It is very important that you don't get caught up comparing yourself to others and focus on the ideal.

So they not only don't support their most gifted employees, they usually find ways to thwart them and "keep them in their place."

This is the difference between a manager and a leader.

MY GREATEST ACCOMPLISHMENT IS WHEN I EMPOWER SOMEONE TO SURPASS ME.

At every point along the path, leaders must understand that they are not the hero, but that their students may be. The coach doesn't make the winning shot; he trains and empowers someone else to.

It's no longer about your personal competence; it's the people you are leading who will accomplish great things.

As a martial arts instructor, I recognize this is the truth for me as well.

As Black Belt Leaders, we need to understand this, too.

Those we are leading will surpass us.

We are building the future.

A leader doesn't fear that process. In fact, if someone says "I want to do what you do," my principles require me to support them. I don't hold them back. I don't fear the passage of time and the growth of my students—I relish it.

My greatest accomplishment is when I produce a student who surpasses me.

THE
TRANSFORMATIONAL
LEADER

As we move into discussing what it means to be a Transformational Leader, it's important to emphasize that Competent Leaders are Black Belts.

They have built their confidence on training with principles as their core. They leverage focus and technique to create momentum.

With a honed ability to focus at will, they embrace opportunities to fail in order to grow and learn—the only way to truly "win." They understand that, in order to achieve, something must be sacrificed.

They have risen above comparing themselves to others, are focused on the ideal, and actively seek to understand how the details relate to the big picture. They are thrilled when one of their "students" surpasses them in skill.

These are the leaders of teams that exceed expectations and find creative, unique solutions to complex challenges. These are the leaders we all want to be around.

They have reached the pinnacle of success—Black Belt.

Now what?

Back to class...

Doing Versus Being

When I finish teaching a class, take off my belt, and put on my regular clothes, do I cease to be a Black Belt?

Do I cease to be an instructor, a *sensei*?

There was a time when teaching karate was just another activity that I did, but that isn't the case anymore.

Almost everyone who starts training in martial arts believes that Black Belt is the end goal.

> "IT'S THE MAN THAT MAKES THE BELT, NOT THE BELT THAT MAKES THE MAN."
>
> –MARTY WEEDON

Nothing could be farther from the truth.

When I earned my Black Belt, I was filled with a sense of knowing that there is so much more to learn.

The final lesson is simple in its complexity.

It boils down to this: with the right training and experience, it is possible to transition from **_doing_** to **_being_**.

I no longer study martial arts; **I AM a martial artist.** I no longer teach karate; **I AM a teacher.**

Let me explain.

In my 30 years of martial arts experience, I've met many different types of students.

One group is typically made up of young people whose parents value the lessons in discipline and control that karate offers. They also understand how impressive achieving the rank of Black Belt looks on a college application. These students come to class much like they would attend scouting meetings or dance classes. They work hard on mastering the skills they will need when they test for Black Belt in much the same way they work toward earning the rank of Eagle Scout or the lead role in the school play.

I've also taught older students who are typically well-established in their careers. They have enough disposable income to indulge in fulfilling the items on their "I've always wanted to…" lists. Much like their younger cohorts, they are disciplined in their workouts and know how to keep their eyes on the prize.

Predictably, both groups work hard at building their arsenal of martial arts skills, and eventually, the vast majority pass their Black Belt test.

They are competent. They are capable. They are Black Belts.

They are justifiably proud of their accomplishment.

But then they disappear.

They've moved on to the next challenge: learning how to sky dive, hiking the Appalachian Trail or climbing Mount Everest.

Although they have achieved much and are incredibly capable, karate is still something that they *do*.

Crossing Over

The next level of leadership requires a commitment to more than skill mastery.

Making this newfound knowledge part of who you *are* instead of just something that you *do* is what will take the competent leader to the next level.

These are the leaders who tap into internal resources to harness external factors and *transform* their situation.

A ***Transformational Leader*** redefines everything that they are involved in.

Not sure what that even means, let alone how it applies to becoming a leader in the Black Belt tradition?

Good, Grasshopper. Knowing that we don't know is the first step.

Most would agree that every quarterback in the National Football League is competent.

They have reached a level of achievement that few ever taste. They are the Black Belts of the sport of football.

Let's look at Peyton Manning, though. In spite of his age and multiple neck surgeries that have weakened his throwing arm, he has done something remarkable.

He has redefined the position of quarterback.

WITH THE RIGHT TRAINING AND EXPERIENCE, IT IS POSSIBLE TO TRANSITION FROM **DOING TO BEING.**

He has changed the way the game is played.

Do you think he turned it off at the end of each season? When he won his first Super Bowl, did he hang up his jersey and move on to the quest of some new goal?

No.

Peyton Manning doesn't just play quarterback. He *IS* a quarterback. Like my instructor Marty Weedon, Peyton Manning is an example of someone who has crossed over into the realm of *being*. Both have moved beyond competence to something far more inspiring.

Both are aware of their innate tendencies and have mastered thousands of skills.

They know how to leverage their strengths and adapt to their weaknesses.

They know what they need to work on to get to the next level, and they seek out opportunities to learn in order to better themselves.

They understand that it is the pursuit of any goal—not the actual achievement of it—that yields the most profound results.

Both are as gracious and accomplished in defeat as they are in victory.

Both have moved from the realm of *doing* to the realm of *being*.

SO HOW DID THEY GET THERE?

It's a riddle, really.

Why would some-
one pursue perfec-
tion, knowing all
along that he or she
will never reach it?

> ## KARATE IS THE PURSUIT OF PERFECTION THAT IS ULTIMATELY FUTILE.
>
> —SCOTT ALEXANDER

Why would anyone set a goal with the full knowledge that it would prove impossible to reach?

Isn't that the ultimate in self-defeating behavior?

Not when you think like a Black Belt.

Students who think like Black Belts gain important insight into this conundrum. While there is no "A-ha!" moment at which the student passes over from Competent to Transformational Leadership, there is a slowly-dawning realization that it is in this very *pursuit* of perfection where they will find the most valuable lessons of all.

This realization is evident as we watch the students who test successful-ly for their Black Belt, and are right back in the *dojo* the very next day.

These are the students who realize something essential about the study of martial arts...

...the destination was not the goal after all.

It's About the Journey

We've all heard this one before: *"Life's a journey, not a destination."* It sounds like a bumper sticker, a cheesy poster in a doctor's waiting room, or an Aerosmith song—but there is a great lesson here with far-reaching implications for leaders in the Black Belt tradition.

In leadership-speak, the process we employ is the journey, and the outcomes we achieve are the destinations.

Now ask yourself this question: If we lead strictly to achieve a given outcome, what does our team do once that happens? If **winning the championship** is our highest ideal, once we win it, there is nothing left to accomplish. But if **pursuit of perfection** is our goal and we move toward it, then winning the championship, while fulfilling, is only a plateau, a stopping point along our journey.

By pursuing the highest ideals, the goals will be achieved as an extension of the process. And new goals will reveal themselves as an extension of the quest for perfection.

Think of a child who is capable at math, and can pass the tests with little effort. Teaching arithmetic skills to a child such as that is secondary. The instructor's higher level goal should be instilling in that child a love of and passion for the subject matter rather than focusing on the achievement of a specific skill set. If this child invests himself and pursues perfection, his skill set will develop along the way.

In similar fashion, championship teams rarely focus on the championship. Rather, they focus on the process—things like goal-setting, team-building and role clarification. Ultimately, with good leadership, the team takes care of the execution, and the goals are achieved as a result of the process—not in spite of the process.

Phil Jackson will go down in history as one of the winningest coaches in NBA history, but he is far more than that. He is a great example of a Transformational Leader.

Coach Jackson tells an interesting story about how he felt at a victory party following the game that clinched the NBA Championship for his team, the New York Knicks, in 1973.

Despite feeling proud of the achievement, Jackson recalls feeling empty. After all the years of practicing and playing, the championship was theirs. The feeling was sweet, but fleeting—and ultimately not that satisfying.

What were they going to do now? Tomorrow would be just another day at work, back on the court.

He recalls feeling that there had to be something more.

Jackson says that moment started him on a journey to do something unheard of in the NBA. He devised a strategy whose ultimate goal was not to win a championship at all costs.

Instead, he set out to lead a team comprised not of individual superstars and a cast of supporting characters, but a network of interconnected talents that would reinvent the way the game was played, and perhaps win championships in the process.

There's a big difference.

And it's easier said than done in the ego-driven arena of professional sports.

A student of Zen and several Native American spiritual traditions, Jackson started by introducing meditation and visualization techniques to his players. His goal was to encourage his players to let go of their own sense of self-importance and see themselves instead as truly important only as integrated parts of a more powerful whole.

These meditation and visualization techniques were a part of Coach Jackson's life. He practiced them every day, vowing that they allowed him to "turn down the noise" in his mind, and focus on "the right here and now, the present moment."

Not surprisingly, this bold approach to the game wasn't immediately embraced—by owners, fellow coaches, sportswriters or fans. At the bottom of the cheering squad were his players.

Before too long, however, Coach Jackson's approach gained a foothold with even the most skeptical players.

This was primarily because of a combination of two things:

First, Jackson's strategies were based on *principle*. In short, they were authentic. What Jackson was asking his players to do was a manifestation of who he was at his core. They were not just a set of exercises with a goal at the end that Jackson had contrived; rather, his new coaching strategies were a key part of who he was as a person.

Second, but just as important, the players had enough respect for Jackson not to walk away.

For example, unlike traditional coaching strategies which rely on the best players handling the ball as much as possible, Jackson equalized court time, giving all the players the same opportunities as the superstars to get their hands on the ball.

PURSUE PERFECTION WITH PRECISION AND INTENTION. ALTHOUGH PERFECTION IS UNATTAINABLE, WE WILL ACHIEVE PERPETUAL TRANSFORMATION.

Despite the outcry, Jackson's team began to act like a team—and the results were solid. Coach Jackson was convinced that leading his players to focus on working together rather than showcasing the greatness of any individual was the path that fused both excellence and achievement.

But the real test of his philosophy came in 1988 when he took a job with the Chicago Bulls, home of Scottie Pippen and perhaps the greatest player the game had ever seen, Michael Jordan.

Instead of simply relying on his superstars, Jackson began leading the Bulls toward becoming one of the most balanced teams in professional basketball.

And incidentally the Chicago Bulls won six NBA championships under Coach Jackson between 1991 and 1998.

But whether we're talking about leadership in the *dojo*, on the basketball court, or anyplace else, it is the **commitment to the pursuit** of perfection that *is* the destination.

The actual *achieving* of perfection is immaterial.

When we make perfection our goal, and move toward it with precision and intention—knowing full well we will never achieve it—we will create something that is far more valuable in the end: *perpetual transformation*.

BUT WHAT IF I DON'T KNOW WHERE I'M GOING?

THE BLIND MEN AND THE ELEPHANT
John Godfrey Saxe

It was six men of Indostan
To learning much inclined,
Who went to see the Elephant
(Though all of them were blind),
That each by observation
Might satisfy his mind.

The First approached the Elephant,
And happening to fall
Against his broad and sturdy side,
At once began to bawl:
"God bless me! but the Elephant
Is very like a WALL!"

The Second, feeling of the tusk,
Cried, "Ho, what have we here,
So very round and smooth and sharp?
To me 'tis mighty clear
This wonder of an Elephant
Is very like a SPEAR!"

The Third approached the animal,
And happening to take
The squirming trunk within his hands,
Thus boldly up and spake:
"I see," quoth he, "the Elephant
Is very like a SNAKE!"

The Fourth reached out an eager hand,
And felt about the knee
"What most this wondrous beast is like
Is mighty plain," quoth he:
"'Tis clear enough the Elephant
Is very like a TREE!"

The Fifth, who chanced to touch the ear,
Said: "E'en the blindest man
Can tell what this resembles most;
Deny the fact who can,
This marvel of an Elephant
Is very like a FAN!"

The Sixth no sooner had begun
About the beast to grope,
Than seizing on the swinging tail

That fell within his scope,
"I see," quoth he, "the Elephant
Is very like a ROPE!"

And so these men of Indostan
Disputed loud and long,
Each in his own opinion
Exceeding stiff and strong,
Though each was partly in the right,
And all were in the wrong!

As early as the 9th century, Buddhist monks, Persian poets, and Hindu statesmen have used variations of this powerful story. As a metaphor, it has been used by scientists to explain everything from wave theory to complicated cell behavior. Children's author Paul Galdone wrote and illustrated a children's book, and animator Richard Williams created an award-winning short film—both based on this ancient parable.

This ancient story found its way into western thinking in the 19th century with this version, credited to John Godfrey Saxe. The phrase "Perception Is Reality" was coined by a German psychologist in the 1920s. English humorist Douglas Noel Adams, best known for *The Hitchhiker's Guide to the Galaxy*, most likely furthered this concept's acceptance with these words:

"Everything you see or hear or experience in any way at all is specific to you. You create a universe by perceiving it, so everything in the universe you perceive is specific to you."

Why has this story persisted in some form or another over hundreds of years?

Probably because it illustrates an essential human behavior: time and time again, a person will base his understanding of the world—his reality, his truth—solely on what he is able to perceive.

In the case of "The Blind Men and the Elephant," although each man touches the same animal, their conclusions about it are wildly different because each bases his conclusions on the limited area he is able to experience, and each is willing to defend his experience as reality.

The poem also makes another important point about perceptions: although often based in fact, they never encompass the complete truth when taken in isolation or out of context.

Remember the big picture?

In the 21st century, many have embraced the concept that "perception is reality."

To those who embrace this world view, there is no right or wrong. Everything is guided by situational ethics—by perceptions, and other subjective data.

THERE ARE ONLY TWO MISTAKES ONE CAN MAKE ALONG THE ROAD TO TRUTH; NOT GOING ALL THE WAY, AND NOT STARTING.

–BUDDHA

TRUTH IS OBJECTIVE – GO FIND IT AND TAKE OTHERS.

In a world where "perception is reality," truth becomes subjective. This way of looking at the world is not only unproductive but patently false. Clearly the elephant is not a tree.

That's why the highest levels of leadership hinge on this realization and this reaction:

Truth is objective. I must go find it and take others with me.

Let's take a moment and discuss a few lessons that can be learned from "The Blind Men and the Elephant."

First of all, the elephant represents truth.

Each of the six wise men arrives at a different conclusion about what the truth looks like based on the one aspect he experiences.

And while each declares his own perceptions to be the truth, those declarations do not make it so. The truth has an objective form that exists in spite of what each man experiences separately.

By being "partly in the right, they all were in the wrong!"

When you lead like a Black Belt, however, you realize: this is not the end of the line. We can uncover the truth if we seek it together. We can compare notes.

Since no one person's perception was complete, sharing their discoveries becomes the path by which the group will be able to assemble the truest picture of the elephant. When we embrace the understandings of others and incorporate them into the whole—instead of defending our perceptions in a vacuum—we will arrive at the most objective and complete truth.

The story of "The Blind Man and the Elephant" does a great job pointing out the need for leaders to commit to an ongoing effort of seeking and defining the truth.

Not as he or she wishes it was.

Not as the marketing department wants to spin it.

Not as it ranks in relation to others.

But as it *is*.

HONG KONG PHOOEY

Throughout my three decades of experience in the martial arts, I can point to several pop culture phenomena that have brought people to my door: Chuck Norris, the Teenage Mutant Ninja Turtles, the Power Rangers, Jackie Chan—just to name a few.

Inspired by these role models, you can imagine how many students brought along with them unrealistic perceptions of what karate could do for them.

Imagine what it was like for those students when they discovered the objective truth about karate training!

> IT IS MY INTEGRITY AND MY ADHERENCE TO PRINCIPLES THAT MAKE ME A TRANSFORMATIONAL LEADER.

In short, students wishing to study karate always show up with a picture in their heads of what it means to be a Black Belt.

Like the "six men of Indostan," these potential students rarely—if ever—have an understanding of the complete truth. Instead, their perceptions are colored by whatever piece of it they have focused on—a TV program, a movie, an action figure set, a cartoon, or a comic book.

In other words, each has a subjective perception that is merely a shadow of the objective truth.

A traditional business approach would dictate that I seek to understand what each potential student is looking for, put a price tag on it, and find a way to deliver the product he or she wants and is willing to pay for.

As a Transformational Leader in the Black Belt tradition, however, I have a different priority. My first goal is to help students discover the objective truth about martial arts and lead them through a process that changes the erroneous picture in their heads.

As a Black Belt Leader, I must always seek to know the largest truth and help others to uncover that truth.

That means I may not deliver the product that they seek and I may lose a prospective student.

This goes back to the concept of winning and losing simultaneously—*yin* and *yang*.

While I may lose a student, I retain my integrity and my reputation.

Ultimately, my integrity and reputation have brought a certain type of student to my door which has allowed me to run a successful karate school for more than 20 years.

Truth is objective, and it doesn't bend to fit the circumstances.

It's not for sale.

I am a **Black Belt** because of my integrity and my adherence to principles.

I am a **Transformational Leader** because of my integrity and my adherence to principles.

"THE SUPREME QUALITY OF LEADERSHIP IS INTEGRITY."

–PRESIDENT DWIGHT D. EISENHOWER

Spinning the Truth

We live in a world where products, concepts, and even people are constantly being marketed to us for others' personal gain.

We're being shown videos and pictures that have been PhotoShopped and edited in order to appear real and to change our perceptions.

Marketing is based on this subtle but very powerful manipulation of our perceptions.

And unfortunately, someone is always trying to manage our perceptions in an effort to manipulate our behavior: to influence our purchasing decision, elicit our votes, or motivate us toward some other type of action or endorsement.

An excellent example of something not being as it appears would be the remarkable sidewalk chalk drawings of Julian Beever.

Using a technique called *trompe l'oeil*, which literally means "trick the eye" in French, Beever uses his drawing skills to create optical illusions.

He specializes in a type of drawing based on deliberate distortion, which—when viewed from the ideal spot—appears to resolve itself into the correct form and shape.

His drawings of pools of water are remarkably realistic. As in any optical illusion, the viewer's mind fills in the details of something with which it is already familiar, effectively duping him into believing the water is real.

This works out fine…until the viewer decides to take a dive into the "pool."

IF PURSUIT OF
PERFECTION IS
THE DESTINATION,

OBJECTIVE
TRUTH

IS SURELY
THE PATH.

That's a potentially painful lesson: Perception is **not** reality.

Magicians rely on this fact to make you see things the way they want you to see them.

Marketers do too.

It's called "spin."

The thing about spin is that it works—but only in the short term.

When you buy into the hype and pay too much for that overpriced product, eventually buyer's remorse will set in. In the long run, you start to distrust that brand and ultimately look for an alternative product that you think is a better value.

As a leader, you never want people to have "buyer's remorse" when they connect with your vision. You minimize that risk when your vision is based on objective truth. As leaders, we must never get caught up in manipulating perceptions and always commit to truth.

Black Belt Leaders seek objective truth, and empower others to do the same.

If pursuit of perfection is the destination, objective truth is surely the path.

PUTTING IT ALL TOGETHER

Aretha Franklin Had It Right

Although I've mentioned respect in various places throughout this book, it's a concept that bears repeating.

As martial artists, the very first lesson we learn is to show respect to our instructors, our fellow students, and the place where we learn our art. While the gesture of bowing may seem trite, it is meaningful, symbolic, and—much like other daily routines that discipline creates—it becomes habit.

Several years ago, Master Weedon started a monthly event called Dog Day. Basically, it is a fighting session that is set to music. I like to explain it as a karate dance. When a new song starts, you find a partner and "dance" (fight) until the song is over. Then you "bow out" and move on to a new partner.

"KARATE BEGINS AND ENDS WITH RESPECT."

–ANKO ITOSU

At least five different martial arts schools are represented each month, and new schools come and go based on their interest. Different martial arts schools take turns hosting the event, so the venue changes constantly.

RESPECT UNDERPINS...

DISRESPECT UNDERMINES.

There are three things, however, that never change. The event is always free, everyone is welcome, and everyone must abide by one rule: no attitude allowed.

Dog Day attracts some of the most accomplished martial artists in the area—top notch fighters. And yet in 25 years, the event has occurred every month without incident.

Sure, there are plenty of bruises and the occasional bloody nose—but no one loses control because the only rule is that *you will respect the other martial artists*—this is the one principle that binds us all together.

There are many lessons to be learned from the success of Dog Day, but I want to focus on ***respect***.

Mutual respect is what makes it possible every month for people of all ages and skill levels to get together and fight with each other without incident.

From a leadership perspective, our bedrock principle must also be respect. Not respect for authority or position, but respect for people and processes. If it's possible to punch someone and throw them on the ground with respect, then it is possible

to confront

to reprimand

to coach

or even fire someone

with respect.

WEAVING YOUR OWN WEB

From Emerging to Competent to Transformational, the levels of leadership covered in this book are not linear. You don't necessarily accomplish one before you move on to the next. In fact, you should be learning and practicing skills from all three at any given time.

Just like the requirements for belts in karate, the levels are convenient as markers for us to gauge our efforts. As a 5th Degree Black Belt with 30 years of experience, guess which *kata* I start my workouts with? That's right—the very first one I learned, a White Belt *kata*!

As a Transformational Leader, when life gives me the opportunity to learn even more (like a new contract at work, or a new student in my class), it propels me back to a new Emergence where my principles, focus, and confidence take center stage to create momentum.

In fact, at any given moment, leaders are drawing from lessons from all three levels or stages simultaneously.

Think of it like a spider web with the levels emanating outward from the center. Every idea, every skill is connected in some way. Every strength, every deficit creates tension somewhere on the web. As we put focus on any spot on the web, the rest of the web is affected in some way—either positively or negatively.

So don't be concerned with identifying exactly where you are on the continuum. You are everywhere at once. You will connect to some concepts more than others. Don't fight it. Just go with it. But remember—all the concepts and principles are intrinsically connected.

Just don't forget to use every concept for your own learning according to your unique strengths and needs.

Leaders—both good and bad—have tremendous impact on our lives. As leaders, this knowledge must drive us to always seek to be better at our craft.

Are you confused? Do you have questions? Remember—that's a good thing. It means you have become more intentionally focused on the idea of leadership.

THE DILEMMA

As mentioned earlier, while it is the new trend to give "10 Easy Steps to… (train your cat, lose five pounds, retire a millionaire)," leadership, like karate, eludes such a simplistic approach.

I can teach you to punch and kick, and you can train until your techniques are impeccable.

But will that make you a great fighter?

This answer to that question is the essence of leadership.

And the answer is "no."

You can't just learn skills. You must learn to be instinctual. You must **become** a fighter.

You can't just learn skills. You must learn to be instinctual. You must **become** a leader.

I once had someone say to me, "By all objective indications, I am a good leader." My response was straight to the point: "Although you may meet all the criteria for good leadership, if you look behind you and no one is following, then the indications are wrong."

During a fight, if I was to ask Marty why he chose one technique over another, he would say, "I don't know—*I just did it.*"

That's the essence of *being* a martial artist. You just do the right thing at the right time—without thinking. It seems instinctual, and yet no one is born with it.

Transformational Leadership is very similar. It appears to be instinctual. It's saying the right thing, and knowing when to keep quiet. It's engaging at the right time, and knowing when to leave it alone.

This type of leader may not be able to explain why he does something, but it ends up being the right call. And while it may seem instinctual, it is actually the product of the thinking and the processes explained throughout this book.

There is no magic formula for becoming an effective leader. Such a thing doesn't exist. There is only your unique raw talent that can be fortified with training and experience in such a way as to infuse it into your essence.

Ultimately, those of us who lead are looking to continually be better at leading. Our path becomes a lifelong pursuit of perfection.

IN
CONCLUSION

EVERYBODY WAS KUNG FU FIGHTING THOSE CATS WERE FAST AS LIGHTNING IN FACT IT WAS A LITTLE BIT FRIGHTENING...

—CARL DOUGLAS (1974)

When two Black Belts who have crossed into the realm of *"being"* compete, it is truly amazing to watch.

I'm not talking about choreographed movie scenes (amazing in their own right), but rather the true martial arts that takes place in dusty old *dojos* every day. The mix of lightning reflexes and power really is a little bit frightening. You get the sense that at any time, someone could be seriously hurt, yet it rarely happens.

Each fighter has trained himself to be in that moment, free of any distractions and connected only to the fight through his mind, body, and spirit. There are no perceptions, only raw talent emboldened by the truth of training and the ability to react and adjust to the other fighter.

The study of karate, the training of the body and mind, the endless practice—all culminates in what can only be called *art*.

Watching a leader who has achieved this same transfer into the realm of *"being"* is equally awesome to behold. Principles, ideals, and strategy are the primary fodder for discussion. The right decisions are made by the right people at the right time. Mistakes are treated as learning opportunities for everyone. Success is shared by all. There is connection and commitment, a sense of being a part of a larger whole. There is ownership. The leader seems to know just what to say (or not say) at the exact right time.

Leadership, like karate, evolves into an art through the complex interaction between your DNA, your focused training, and your experience.

As leaders, we have a profound impact on the people around us. It is a responsibility that we must take very seriously.

Every interaction we have holds the opportunity to empower another person—to propel them forward on their journey toward perfection.

Every interaction we have holds the opportunity to deny another person—to stymie their personal journey.

Empower or deny?

The choice is simple, but the path seldom is.

LEADERSHIP, LIKE KARATE, EVOLVES INTO AN ART THROUGH THE COMPLEX INTERACTION BETWEEN YOUR DNA, YOUR FOCUSED TRAINING, AND YOUR EXPERIENCE.

By now it should be clear: the essence of leadership is a lifelong pursuit. It begins with your unique talents, proceeds according to your experience… and it never ends.

There is no magic formula, but the key ingredients to growth along this path have been revealed throughout this book. As experience continues to hand you opportunities for growth, look for ways to apply the concepts reflected in these "Nuggets of Wisdom." Over time, this is what will move you along the path toward Transformational Leadership.

THE ESSENCE

LEADERSHIP PERSPECTIVES

- Leadership, like karate, evolves into an art through the complex interaction between your DNA, your focused training, and your experience.

- With the right training and experience, it is possible to transition from *doing* to *being*.

- It is my integrity and my adherence to principles that makes me a Transformational Leader.

REDEFINED SUCCESS

- The desired outcome isn't winning or losing—it's learning.

- Ultimately, *winning* or *losing* is arbitrary—and almost always fleeting.

- In any dynamic interaction—at any given moment—we are both winning and losing at the same time.

- The only way to fail is to give up.

- My greatest accomplishment is when I empower someone to surpass me.

THINKING LIKE A BLACK BELT

- Respect underpins…disrespect undermines.

- When we change our thinking, we control our actions. By controlling our actions, we change our circumstances.

- When we leave our comfort zone, we become more focused. Being confused or unsure can be a good thing. Embrace opportunities to be confused.

- Look for the opportunities to be hit, kicked, and knocked to the ground. This is where you will learn the most.

- It is the big picture that makes the details relevant.

- If pursuit of perfection is the destination, objective truth is surely the path.

- Confidence isn't the absence of fear—it's being able to take action in spite of fear.

HABITS OF BLACK BELT LEADERS

- Pursue perfection with precision and intention. Although perfection is unattainable, we will achieve perpetual transformation.

- Truth is objective—go find it and take others.

- Compromise on strategies, not principles.

- Like the student trying to learn a new kick, focusing in on the smallest pertinent detail of any project without distractions can yield astounding results.

- Work in short bursts of intense focus.

- Learn to flip the switch: change your focus quickly, completely, and at will to move nimbly between situations or interactions.

- Compare everything to the ideal. Once we settle for anything less, we are on a fast track to mediocrity.

- Seek balance between the big picture and the ideal in order to make sense of your current situation and determine priorities.

EPILOGUE

It doesn't matter who we are.

Life is going to throw us some curveballs.

We may not realize it right away, but inside every one of those curve-balls is an opportunity. It may be disguised as one of our worst night-mares coming true, but it is there if we look hard enough.

And once we recognize the opportunity within the curveball, we have a choice: Do we dig in and knock it out of the park, or step out of the box and watch it sail by?

How we deal with the opportunities that come our way is one of the most defining elements of our journey.

I know that was the case with me.

Several years ago, I made the choice to resign from a position as CEO. Within two months of choosing my principles over a pay-check, my father passed away unexpectedly.

In the months that followed, many people came forward to offer their condolences, and to tell me what they remembered about him. As I lis-tened to the things people were saying, I had a life-changing realization.

Although my father had been a well-known businessman in the community, that wasn't what people remembered about him. Instead, the stories people told me—while all very different—had one thing in common: they were all about the **impact** my father had on them.

It wasn't my father the accountant they remembered; it was the little league baseball or football coach from years ago. It wasn't the business man; it was the Lion's Club volunteer. What remained in people's memories was the human being who had been willing to share his time and talent to assist someone else along on their journey.

Without a doubt, my father's passing was one of my curveballs. I had to look long and hard to find the opportunity.

Over the next year, I received several job offers. They offered stability and room for advancement, but I came to realize that they were not for me.

My life needed to be about impact. My challenge was to find a way to use my unique skills, abilities, and experiences to assist other people on their journeys. So I walked away from the more traditional job offers and started down a new road that led me to writing the book you have just read.

I had found the opportunity.

I took a swing rather than watch it sail by.

Acknowledgements

I would like to express my gratitude to all who have supported me through the process of writing this book: the entire team at MMG, especially Joanne McCoy for going above and beyond; my wife, Cathy, for her expert guidance; and Mimi Zee for being part of my team.

I would be remiss if I didn't thank those who kicked me around and made me the martial artist I am today: Marty Weedon, Brian McKoy, Mark Alexander, Ryan "Zip-Zip" Zimmerman, and the rest of the old-school Golden Knights.

To those who continue to motivate me: Mackensie "Big Mac" Smith, Andy Eskander, Jim & Aimee Massey, and Mark Keefer.

To all the parents who have trusted me with their kids for all these years—thank you for sharing them with me. I have learned much from them.

Thank you to all my work colleagues over the years who truly understood the value of being principled.

And, finally, to my dad—in more ways than one, the reason this book exists.

Invitation

Scott Alexander is a speaker, consultant, and coach who draws on his experiences in martial arts and business to guide individuals and organizations on their unique paths to creating maximum impact. Interested in getting Scott involved in the leadership discussion at your organization? You can reach him at:

Email: LeadLikeABlackBelt@gmail.com

Facebook: Lead Like a Black Belt

Twitter: Scott Alexander@LikeaBlackBelt

Website: www.ScottMAlexander.com